Breakable Unbreakable

*My T*ruth and Lies of Sexual Abuse

Latoya Dukes

Life Chronicles Publishing
Give your life a voice!

http://www.mylifechronicles.org
Life Chronicles Publishing
ISBN-13:978-0998911489
ISBN- 10: 0998911488
Cover Design:
Adrian Sims
Editor:
Lisa Maki
Life Chronicles Publishing Copyright © 2017

Contents

Introduction

Acknowledgement

Introduction

There is nothing like looking at yourself in the mirror every day knowing that what you see is not what people see. While others see you as this strong person, what you see is a scarred woman, broken from all the sexual assaults that have happened to her. You put on that fake smile, while deep inside you are crying out for help.

While I was good in consoling those who have been raped or sexually assaulted, there I was with no one to talk to about the sexual abuse I endured. I wanted to say, "You don't even know me. You don't even know what I've been through."

Then, one day, you finally wake up and decide that it's time for you to change and tell the whole world about your story. At last, you want to be free and live free.

Breakthrough the unbreakable with me and be free!

Acknowledgments

To all the women and men who have experienced sexual assaults: May this book help empower you to live free and tell your truth. May we all be able to walk together, not as victims but as victors, using our experience to help others.

To my husband: Thank you for being with me through the hardest time of my life, and for being patient with me even when I felt like giving up.

To my sister Leticia: Thank you for pushing me to continue to write and finish this book until the end.

To my parents: I love you guys. Writing this was not easy for me, but you stuck with me 100%. I love you and thank you for everything.

To my siblings: I love you guys.

To my children: As you get older and can read my story, just know that mommy loves you, and you are one of the most important reasons why I am still here to write this book.

To my best friend Keri: Thank you for listening to me cry and weep and cry some more. This was one of the hardest things for me to do, but you stayed with me.

To my cousin Brianna: I love you, and I thank God that you pushed me to continue to keep my faith.

Chapter One
Blinded by The Age of Five

I was a shy and quiet type of a kid. I loved watching cartoons, playing toys and with my siblings. I didn't mind playing by myself though. In fact, I preferred it that way because it was not easy for me to ask kids if they wanted to play with me. I always waited for them to ask to play first. Going to the community center and watching my brother play basketball was my favorite thing to do; my older sister would let me tag along with her and her friends. A lot of the times she didn't have a choice because she had to watch me and keep up with me. Our mother back then was tied up with being on drugs, so she was not really around. My older sister took care of me when I was little, so she was like my other mom when my mom was not around.

I was five years old, my mom had this boyfriend who I really loved. He would make me laugh and would even play Barbies with me. One-day, he told me that we were going to play a game. Man, oh man, did I love playing games. He explained to me this was a new game and that this game was going to be a lot of fun. However, in this game, we could not tell anyone what we do or what the game is about. "This game will be our little secret," he said.

I couldn't wait to play this new game. I was so excited that I asked if we can play right there and then. He told me yes and that I had to get up on the bed and lay down to play. My mom at the time was not home, and my siblings were at school. It was still bright outside, and the sun was out. It was a nice day, but he said we were playing inside. I went to the bedroom and laid on the bed. He came in and pulled my pants down.

"Why do my pants have to be down to play this game?" I asked.

"This is a special kind of game," he said. "It's like a game of doctors, but you don't tell anyone what we are playing."

He then began to abuse me sexually. I told him to stop because I didn't like the game.

"Just be quiet and relax. This game is fun; all little girls like it."

Not me. I didn't like the game. He placed his hands over my mouth to make sure I wouldn't be loud or yell.

"Please stop. It hurts," I remember telling him.

He whispered in my little ear, "Just relax and close your eyes; it's okay."

He didn't listen to me. This game was supposed to be fun, but to me, this game was not fun at all. After he was done, he then told me to remember that this game was a special one and that no one was allowed to know about it. He warned me that if I say anything to anyone about this game I would be in big trouble and I wouldn't be able to see my family again.

He pulled his pants up and left the room. I went to my room, and I cried very quietly so that no one would hear me. I made sure before I came out of my room that I cleaned my face up because I didn't want anyone to know. I was afraid of not seeing my family ever again. For the rest of the night, I acted as normal as I could.

As he smiled at me and winked at me from across the room, I just smiled, but deep down I wanted to scream. I wanted to tell everyone that we played a game, that was not fun at all, but I didn't say anything. I pretended everything was fine even as I felt this stabbing sensation down in my abdomen. I guess the physical pain was more bearable than the emotional and mental trauma it caused me. My very young mind could not understand how a little girl like me can enjoy a game like that.

I woke up the next day barely wanting to get up and walk because the feeling felt even worse than the day it happened. I lied to my sister and told her that I wasn't feeling well so that I didn't have to go to school. Then my mom's boyfriend came in the door, and I told my sister that I changed my mind and that I was going to school.

When I came home that afternoon, my mom's boyfriend, Joe, was still there. She said she had to go to the store and asked him if he can watch over me. He agreed excitedly, and I begged my mom to take me with her.

"No, I don't feel like taking you with me," my mom said.

"I'll watch her; don't worry about it. You go ahead," he said.

My mom grabbed her things and closed the door behind her.

All I could think in my mind was, "Please don't let him touch me again; it hurts."

"Come on Latoya, let's go play our special game," Joe said.

"I don't want to play the game. I want to watch TV in the living room."

"Nope. We are going to your mom's room, and we are going to play the game."

He then grabbed my hand and took me into my mom's room and laid me on the flower blanket with pink roses. He started to play "doctor" all over again. He held me down because I was so fidgety and wanted to get out of the room.

"If you don't relax and be a good girl, you will never see your family again," he said.

I just laid there, and I remember the tears rolling down my face. After it was over, he smiled and said, "the game is over for now but remember, you cannot tell anyone because you know what will happen if you do." He placed his index finger on his lips and said, "shhh, it's our little secret."

As time passed by, Joe just disappeared. It turned out that he was also touching my older sister. She was crying one day when a close friend of hers asked what was wrong. She told him, and the authorities got called. They took Joe into custody.

He ended up having a trial for what he did to my sister. However, my mother told her to plead the 5th, so the charges against him were dropped. He went to jail for only a few days and didn't end up in prison for the crime he committed. You have to remember that at that time, our mother was obviously not in the right frame of mind.

I never told my mom and sister what happened to me because even when they were going to court, I didn't understand what was happening. I was just a kid, and all

I wanted to do was go home and play with my toys. And, I was still afraid of his threat that if I told anyone, I would never be able to see my family again.

Finally, at the age of 24, I told my mom and older sister that he touched me too. They were both shocked and asked why I never said anything. I told them that I was scared of his threat and that I was so confused about what was going on when they were in court. Little did I know that this was just the beginning of my story, and I had an even longer journey ahead of me.

Reflection

•At what age did you get blinded?

•Are you afraid today to speak your truth about sexual

abuse? If so, use this page to journal your pain until you

can verbalize the pain inside.

Chapter 2
Telling My Truth Is Real

Some people say that your family is the closest to your heart and the ones you can trust the most. How I wish this were the case with me. Unfortunately, the opposite happened.

I was six years old when a family member took advantage of my trust in him. As a kid, all I wanted to think of was being happy, and that's what this guy made me feel in the beginning. He was very funny, and he always made me laugh. I looked up to him as a father, since I didn't have one growing up. He was the one person who would tell me to toughen up if I fell and started to cry, or who would make me laugh instead of cry. He also loved picking me up and putting me on his shoulders. I loved being up high because I could see everything, including tall buildings, bright green trees, and the traffic on the roadways.

Things turned out bad when this man started to touch me. He would pick me up by the private and arm and would pull me up to his shoulders. While I was there, he would take his fingers and fondle me, telling me not to say a word. I do not know what he was thinking, and why he would think that it was okay for him to do that. It was not okay. I was only six years old.

Just like my mom's boyfriend, this man made me believe that if I told anyone, no one would believe me anyway. They would all just think that I was a dramatic little girl. So, for many years I blocked out this memory. I never wanted to believe for a moment that someone who I love so dearly could do something like that. I made myself think that it was a bad dream I had and that it never happened to me. I continued to live in this phase of denial as I grew older.

One day, as I was talking to my cousin, the truth came out of my mouth. I can't believe that something I made myself forget and made myself believe was just a dream came out of my mouth! It finally hit me that everything was real. Not only did it come out of my mouth, but it shocked me. Finally, after holding something like that in for so long, the real truth came out.

Now my cousin knew this person very well. She knew that when I said it, I wasn't lying. She looked at me and told me she believes it and that she believes me. That made me really think that maybe if I would have said something years ago that others would have believed me as well. But that wasn't the case.

I ended up telling my older sister and my mom who both believed me and asked why I waited for so long to say something. I told them that I blocked this memory out for years and thought that it was just a bad dream and that I didn't want to say it was true. A few weeks after I told my mom and sister, I believe God told me to make a video and post it on Facebook. It was not a video of me saying who touched me but a video of me saying that I also am a sexual assault and molestation victim and survivor. I want other women to know that I am here for them and for them to see that they are not alone. I made the video, and I posted it. I never mentioned any names of anyone or of what they did.

Well, word got out about my video, and someone ends up calling my family, freaking out, and telling them to tell me to stop lying and that I'm a bitch who needs to stop trying to play a victim. I get a phone call asking me what was going on and why I would make a video like that. I told them I made the video for other victims to know that their truth is real... that they are not alone... that there are others in this world, who are like them. My family was pretty upset with me because I never told them anything about me being sexually assaulted or being molested as a kid. They also loved this family member, and they didn't want to believe that I was telling the truth. Another family member got so angry with me and refused to believe me. I was told that I sounded like I needed to be in a psych ward and that making up things like that was not funny. They said that if it really happened to me, I wouldn't have waited this long to say something. I again explained that I blocked it out for so many years and convinced myself that it was a bad dream.

There I was thinking to myself, why didn't believe me. I didn't understand why I was the one hurting and why I was the one shedding tears. Nobody wanted to believe me except the women that had been through what I had endured. I knew I was not crazy. I knew the truth. What I could not understand was why they couldn't appreciate MY truth and why they can't believe me.

As this was going around, word got back to that man, and so he started telling people that I was lying and that he would never ever touch me. I cried and cried. I even tried to tell those closest to me that he was lying because when we were younger, another girl also claimed that he touched her and tried to rape her. However, no one could remember that. I understood that some of my family couldn't remember; I knew some could but chose not to recall because of the love for this person. I think they wanted it to go away and thought that I would be able to get over it someday.

After a while, I decided to just cut those closest to me off because I knew My truth and I knew what I said was real. Eventually, I got an apology, explaining that they just didn't understand. My family was hurt because they felt as if I should have told them first before posting it on social media. I forgave them, but some still to this day believes that it didn't happen to me and that I was lying. Yes, some are still very confused on how or why, or if I'm even telling the truth.

After a month of crying and regretting that I even said anything, I finally made my head stop spinning. The 'beating myself up' came to an end. Everyone else continued to live their lives as if my truth was not real. As for me, I know my truth is real, and I stuck to it. By telling the whole world about it, I was set free from the lie I made myself believe. I awakened from a dream that I was living in. I finally admitted to myself that it really did happen to me. It doesn't matter anymore that the man who did it to me called me a liar. I stand by My truth and will continue to do so.

Reflection

Answer these questions honestly, and let your answers help you bring out your truth.

•Have you ever been told that you are a liar and not a victim of sexual abuse or assault?

•What do you do with these feelings?

•Do you have support outside of family to help you with your truth? If no, please seek outside counsel and support.

Chapter 3
Blaming Myself

Being a teenager is different from being a little kid. You go through middle school experiences like, get curious about boys, hanging out with friends, and develop crushes.

I was still shy when I became a teenager. However, my smile would always light up the room. Once I did talk, I was the most outgoing person, and people really liked me. I loved going to church, and that's where I met one of my ex-boyfriends. We will just call him Tyler. Tyler was really cute and would make me laugh. He was older than me by two years, was very tall, had lots of hair, and he was very handsome. His skin glowed, and his teeth sparkled when he smiled.

Tyler invited me to his 17th birthday party, a day that I will never forget. I got dropped off by my mom at the cabana where he was having his party. When I got inside, the DJ was playing music, and there were people everywhere. I walked around for about ten minutes looking for Tyler when I finally found him. He said hi, but he barely stayed with me because he was so busy entertaining friends; I basically hung out with his family. After the party was over, I ended up staying the night with Tyler because I couldn't find a ride home. Besides, church was the next day, so Tyler's grandma said that she would pick us up in the morning to go to church with her. We got into Tyler's house, and we decided to watch movies and cuddle; there was kissing involved, of course. I ended up falling asleep, and I remember it was the crack of dawn when Tyler woke me up, telling me to come into his room and lay with him. I went and lied down. We started making out and getting all aroused. I didn't know what that feeling was because I was still a virgin; all I knew was that it felt good at that moment. Tyler put on a condom, and he got on top of me, asking if he could stick his penis inside of me. I said yes, and we started slowly having sex. I asked him to stop because it hurt. He told me to relax and that it was going to hurt because it was my first time. I tried to relax but I couldn't. Again, I told him to stop and that I didn't want to do it anymore because it hurt so bad; Tyler insisted. He took my hands, held them above my head, and held them down; then he put his hand over my mouth and started humping away. As I laid there crying with tears rolling down my cheeks, his whole body was on top of me. I could not move. I was so numb and hurt that all I could do was cry. I wondered if anyone would hear me if I tried to scream. Everything around me felt so cold.

I walked quietly to the bathroom after Tyler was done. I didn't want to make any noise because his mom was already sleeping in her room with his baby brother and little sister. My legs felt like Jell-O as I sat down on the toilet; all I felt was pain. I peed and wiped; there was a bunch of blood. I started to panic because I was scared and didn't know why there was blood coming out of me. I wanted to cry some more and scream, but nothing came out. I was so hurt and so numb on the inside that nothing felt real around me. I didn't want to believe that Tyler raped me. I just wanted to think that it was both our fault. I just kept saying to myself, "It's your fault because you said yes and that you wanted to do it. You should have said no when he asked the first time." I finally came out of the bathroom after cleaning myself up and went to lie back down on the couch. Tyler came out and asked me if I was okay, but I could not even open my mouth to say anything to him. He went back to his room to lie down. A few hours later, Tyler's grandma called and said that she was on the way to pick us up. I got up to get dressed. Tyler told me not to say anything about what happened that morning. I just looked at him and got in the car. His mom was still asleep when we left.

It was dead silent as we drove to church. His grandma must have noticed it, so she turned up her church music. As we sat there in church, I was still so confused, and my emotions were all over the place. "Do I tell someone? Do I stay silent? Do I scream it out? Should I not say anything because nobody is going to believe me? Will they just think that I'm lying and that I was the one who wanted sex?" All these questions were going on in my head at the same time.

Tyler's grandma drove me home after church. She asked how the party was; I said it was good. She asked why I was so quiet; I said I was tired. The look in her eyes showed that she didn't believe me. The remaining conversation went this way.

"Where did you sleep?" she asked.

"On the couch," I responded.

"And where did Tyler sleep?"

"In his room," I said.

She looked at me straight into my eyes and said, "You guys better not be having sex." I was dumbfounded, and scared. I knew that she knew.

As we were pulling up to my house, she put the car in park and said, "I know you did," and she started getting so upset. She asked Tyler questions and got back to me for some answers. "I told him to stop and that I didn't want to anymore, but he wouldn't." She yelled at Tyler and asked, "Tyler, did she ask you to stop?" Tyler said yes, and she asked why he did not stop.

"Because she wanted to have sex too just as I did," he said.

"No, I told you to stop, but you didn't. You kept going and held me down," I said.

"So, you raped her!" Grandma yelled even louder this time.

"No grandma. I wouldn't do that," Tyler said.

I was too shocked to say anything.

Tyler's grandma looked at me and said, "You and Tyler can no longer be together, and you can no longer communicate with each other. You will not talk about this, and we will live our lives as nothing happened. At this point, I do not know who to believe. Is that understood?"

I still couldn't say a word. I was still in shock. I was sweating and breathing heavily.

"Did you understand?!?" Grandma yelled.

I just shook my head and slowly got out of the car. I walked towards my front door and looked back to see them drive off. Back home, I snapped back to reality, pretending like nothing happened. I just wanted to erase everything from my mind, yet I saw it. It kept playing over and over again. When I closed my eyes, it was there.

I never saw Tyler again after that. He stopped coming to church, and his grandma moved to a different one. I went back to blocking things out, pretending that it never happened. By that time, I was already good at forgetting all the painful things. As far as I knew, my life went on as if it wouldn't ever happen

again. That's what I thought.

Reflections

•Did you ever blame yourself or trick yourself into believing that what happened to you was your fault?

Journal your feelings.

Chapter 4
His Lies Vs. My Truth

A church hurt is the most unbearable hurt you could feel in your life. It makes you want to turn away from God, church, people, and the Bible. Going through this church hurt made me feel like I could not go on any longer. I just wanted to die and never see another day. You go through a roller coaster ride of emotions: days when you feel sad, days when you think you are happy, but you're really just trying to hide the pain in your heart. I felt so betrayed and alone.

It all started when I got a call from my pastor one day saying he needed a friend to talk to. He couldn't speak to his wife because she was pregnant, and he didn't want to stress her out. Being the loving and caring person that I am, I agreed to meet with him. He wanted to meet the next day, and he told me not to tell anyone that I was meeting up with him. I should have already seen that as a red flag, but no, I was the same vulnerable person who still believed the best in people, no matter how much abuse I had already received back then. However, I thought of other things like what if an accident happens or somebody kills me, and nobody knew where I was. I decided to tell my husband where I was going. Though he told me that it was not a good idea, I was able to convince him that everything was going to be fine. We trusted our pastor anyways.

I got a call at around 5 pm the next day from our pastor. He asked if I was still coming to meet him and I said yes. When I got to the church, no one was there. I went and knocked on his office door. He opened it, let me in, and asked me to sit down. I chose the chair across from him. He then told me that he didn't want to talk to me in his office because he wanted me to see him as an average person, not as a pastor. I thought nothing was wrong with that, so I agreed. We got up, and I followed him as he walked down the hall of the church and into the children's room. "Let's talk here," he said, pointing to a closet. I was shocked and said, "You want to talk in there?" He freaked out and said, "I knew I couldn't trust you," and he started to get frustrated. I got scared, but I kept calm because I knew what a man like him could do, considering the past molestations and assaults I've endured. I was thinking of my children at that point, so I didn't yell, scream, or freak out. I followed him into the closet and there were two chairs: a couch and a computer chair. I noticed some butterflies on the wall and a computer desk. He told me he didn't want the big light on, so he only left the small reading light on. I was scared! My mind started racing, and I was having flashbacks of being molested as a kid. He began to talk to me about normal life and the stress that he has been having. He began to share with me stories about how stressed his wife was and about the things they were going through. From there, things started to get a little weird. He asked if I can just hold him and give him a hug because he needed one. "I will turn my body around, so you can hug me from behind, so it won't feel and look weird for you," he said. "I don't know about that. I don't want to feel like I'm cheating on my husband or committing adultery," I responded. "Come on; we are just friends. I won't make it weird. I just need a friend at this point."

I was very scared. My heart was pounding so hard; I could hear my heartbeat. My mind was on my kids. At that point all I could think of was, "I have to go back to my kids." I walked over to the couch chair he was sitting on and hugged him from behind. He moved around and there we were face to face. He told me to hug him more, and I got even more scared. He started to hold me and breathed on my neck. He kept asking, "Are you comfortable enough?" I said, "I think we should get up." "No," he said, "Just a little while longer, I just need a friend."

I then started to feel his penis getting hard on my leg. I jumped up and told him that things are getting weird and that it was time to get out of the closet. He began to freak out again saying he knew he couldn't trust me and rubbed his head. I told myself to keep calm if I want to go back to my kids. "I want to ask you something, but I don't know if I can trust you," he said.

"You can trust me, what is it?" I replied. He said that he never had someone do certain sexual favors on him and that his wife is not up to doing crazy things like that. He then asked, "Will you?" I was stunned! I said, "No, I will not do that. Don't you understand that's adultery? I will never cheat on my husband. That's not me." He got frustrated, and I asked if we can finally leave the closet, and he said we could. As we were getting out of the closet, I made sure to remain calm. I wasn't sure if he was going to yell at me or attack me, so I didn't want to trigger anything. I just smiled and kept walking. He then went back to pastor mode and apologized for doing such a thing, and that he didn't know where that side of him came from. He asked if we can just forget about what happened in the closet.

Tears poured down my face as again he said, "I'm so sorry. Please don't cry. I will never do that again." I remained calm as he told me not to tell anyone because it could ruin him. "I am not that kind of person," he said. He begged me to forgive him and asked that I do not tell anyone and I agreed to do so. All I wanted at that time was to leave and get back to my kids alive. "This will never ever happen again," I told him sternly. He promised that it won't. He finally let me go, so I got in my car and drove home.

As I was driving down the road, the shock hit me like a rock. I could not believe it. He was supposed to be my shepherd, my pastor, and someone I went to for guidance. I kept asking God, "Why me Lord, why? "Why out of everyone did he choose me for such a horrible act? I was so hurt and was in such a panic. Thoughts started to run wild in my mind. "What do I do? Should I tell my husband? But he is not a big fan of church. He just opened his heart to Christ. I don't want to ruin that."

I called my husband and lied to him. I told him that the talk was about the pastor's life, nothing so big. My husband believed me but then asked, "Why do you sound weird?" I panicked and thought of something quickly to say. "I'm just very tired; it's been a long day." I finally got to my kids, picked them up, and drove home.

I was still sick to my stomach when I got to my house. I hopped in the shower feeling disgusted and dirty; I started scrubbing my body off like there was so much dirt on me that would not come off. It was hard falling asleep. Thoughts of him coming to my house and breaking in kept me awake.

The next day came, my phone rang and it was him checking on me and apologizing for what happened in the closet. I told him that I didn't want to talk about it anymore. He agreed. I continued to go to church, and I bet you are asking yourself why. Well, I serve God and not man. If I stopped going to that church, my husband would be suspicious, which was what I was avoiding. I also went back because I worked in the preschool at the church and we did not have substitutes who could take my place. Leaving those kids who I have built a relationship with and even bonded with, was not an option for me. When he came around me, I got the chills and felt dirty. Yet, I knew I had to hold it together for the sake of peace around me.

He called me almost every day when my husband was not home but would not call when he was home. He knew his schedule so well. A week went by, and we were having problems with our preschool. He called me and asked if he could come to my home and talk to me about the changes he has made to the school. My husband was not home yet because he had to stay overnight at work and the pastor knew that. Reluctantly, I said he could come to discuss his new plans.

My kids were in bed when I got a knock on the door at 8:30 pm. I let him in and asked him to take a seat. I sat across from where he was. "Why are you sitting so far away? I feel very uncomfortable," he said. "Come sit beside me," he added. "I'm fine sitting here." "Come here. No one's here anyway," he said. I got scared and had flashbacks from the closet. My kids were upstairs; my husband was at work. All I could think of was to keep myself and my kids safe. I moved closer to him because I didn't want him to flip out and do something crazy. Again, I remained calm. He went on and talked about the preschool and why the parents were not bringing their kids to class on the days that I would work. He then changed the subject and started to get sexual with me. He started to breathe down my neck and asked me what my husband and I do in the bedroom. I began to shake. I didn't want to scream and wake the kids up. So, I told him the things that I do to my husband, and he started to feel on me. "Please stop," I said. "Come on, it's okay," he said. He touched my breasts, my private, and my bottom. I begged him to stop. He asked if I would do a sexual favor for him and I said no. He got a little upset and told me that he just wanted a little bit. I started to pray that my husband would call and within 30 seconds my phone rang. He jumped up and fixed his pants. He asked me if my husband calls around at that time and I said yes. He got nervous and left. I talked to my husband and remained calm. I didn't know how to tell him what just happened.

The next day I went to my best friend's house and told her everything. I couldn't hold it in any longer. One more minute of keeping it to myself and I will end up committing suicide. When I got to her house and pulled up, I sat in the car for a second. I was scared of what her reaction would be, or if she would even believe me. What if she doesn't believe me? "Okay LaToya, get it together. You trust her so go in there and tell her," I told myself. I got out of the car and rang the doorbell. She opened the door, and we exchanged hugs. She sat me down and asked me what was going on. I told her everything, and she was so angry she wanted to kill him herself. The whole time we were talking he kept calling and texting my phone because I had been ignoring him all day. She then grabbed my phone and put it face down. She asked me if I was okay and told me that she believed me and that there wasn't a moment in the whole story that she didn't believe me. I told her how I hadn't told my husband yet because I was too scared of what he was going to say or what he will think. Most importantly, I didn't want him to go and kill someone and be in prison for the rest of his life.

Tears streamed down my face because I just couldn't keep myself together. She told me that she would talk to her husband about it and then we arranged to not go to church that Thursday so that I could tell my husband with their support. I thanked and hugged her, and I went home. My phone was still blowing up, and I finally answered and told him that I was going to tell my husband about what he did to me. He started panicking and crying, begging me not to tell because he was afraid of his wife finding out. He claimed that he didn't remember everything that happened but that he was so sorry. I told him I had to go and hung up the phone.

My husband came in the door from work, and I gathered myself together, pretending like nothing was wrong. He kept asking if I was okay and I said yes. Finally, Thursday came. I called up the church and told them that I was not going to be there that night. As for my husband, I told him we were going to my friend's house for dinner. While we were in the car, the kids were loud and argued in the back seat, but it was as though everything was silent around me. You know when you can hear your heart thumping from inside of your chest. That's all I could hear because I was so nervous. We got to their house, went inside, and got the kids situated before we sat down. They looked at me, and I gave them the okay look, and I took a deep breath and told him everything.

As I began to tell him what had happened, his eyes got crazier and crazier. After I was done, he looked at me and said, "Why didn't you tell me?" I said, "I was too afraid, and I didn't want you to go to prison." He said he didn't care that we were going to church. He just wanted to kill him. We calmed him down. He told me that he believed me, but at the same time wondered how a 25-year old married woman could have let something like that happen. I told him that during those moments all I could do was sit in panic in my head. All I kept thinking was to keep myself alive for our children. I also explained to him that it brought back flashbacks of my past, of being molested and raped as a kid, and I stood there frozen in time. He said he was sorry that it happened to me and he started to blame himself for not being here to protect me. I told him that it was not his fault and that I should have read all the signs, but I was just so blinded. We stayed at our friend's house for a bit just to make sure he was calmed down; then we ended up going home.

On the drive back home, he just kept looking at me and holding and kissing my hand, and I just kept smiling at him to let him know that I was okay. Yet, deep down I was not okay. I just wanted him to be okay and I didn't want him to hurt anyone. I understood why he felt the way he did.

The next day the pastor called my phone, and I told him my husband knew what he did to me. He tried to play his humble card and then told me I had a right to tell him and asked if he could meet up with my husband and me at our home. My husband told him to come over, but I knew it was going to be a bad idea.

I remember warning him that he may not be able to hold back from hurting the pastor, but he said that he wanted to hear his side of the story. It was not that he didn't believe me; he just wanted to see if he was going to lie to try and save himself. The pastor ended up coming over. As soon as he pulled up to the driveway, I went right back to the flashbacks. His face kept playing in my mind. I put my phone on record mode, so I can record the whole conversation. I knew he was going to flip it on me. And even if he decided to confess and tell the truth, I realized it was still good to record everything.

My husband decided to sit on a chair behind the couch. He said he needed to keep a distance just in case he felt like killing him. We all sat down, and the pastor began to apologize for what he did. He admitted that he touched me and that he was sorry for his actions. My husband gave him two options: either he tells his wife what he did, or my husband will tell her.

"No, please don't do that. Please don't tell my wife," the pastor begged. "Is there a way we can work around this? I can't tell her this. She will be devastated. "If you couldn't tell her, then you shouldn't have done what you did," my husband responded.

The pastor didn't care. He just kept pleading not to tell his wife. My husband warned him, "I will give you three days. If you don't tell her, I will tell her."

He stood up and decided to leave. Before walking out the door, he asked if he could hug us. My husband looked at him like he was insane. He finally left.

A day later, I got a phone call from my best friend saying that she told one of the deacons of the church who happened to be our good friend. When she told him about the incident, he already knew. He said that God gave him a dream a week ago but that he didn't know how to approach me about it. He ended up calling me to ask my side of the story, and if he could just come over to the house to talk about it in person. I agreed, and he came over the next day.

We let him in, and I asked him about his dream, as I was very curious. He told me that he dreamed about the whole closet part, but he didn't know how to approach me about it. Obviously, God gave him that dream for a reason. What I couldn't understand was why God would send a dream to someone after it already happened, and not before the incident to serve as a warning. I was too shocked to say anything. He then got up and said that he was going to talk to the pastor to hear his side of the story and to see if he will lie or tell the truth. I then told him that I recorded the pastor's confession. He looked appalled as he sat there and listened to the recording. He asked me to send it to him, so he can tell the pastor that he can't lie. With grief on his face, he said sorry for what happened to me and that we will keep in touch.

I stopped going to church from then on. I was too sick to my stomach to look at that man. Besides, my husband just wanted to kill him, so it was best for us to stay away. A few days went by, and we got a call from the deacon that the pastor denied everything. "What matters is that I know the truth," the deacon said. "I made him tell his wife, and I am calling you to see if we could all sit down and have a meeting because his wife wants to know your side of the story." I was dead silent. I thought to myself, "Why do we need to keep reliving this situation over and over again? I just want it to stop and go away." After a long pause, he said, "hello, are you there?" I snapped out of it, and I agreed to the meeting for as long as he and my husband will be there with me.

We got to the church in the evening of the next day, while service was going on. Somebody else was leading it. We walked over to the meeting room, and I sat from across the pastor's wife, while my husband sat across from the pastor. The deacon stayed in the corner.

"Now tell me your side of the story because I've already heard his'," the pastor's wife said. I began to tell everything, and after I was done, she said, "Wow, this story is very detailed." I said, "Yes, I am a very detailed person." "I don't believe you," she retorted. "First, it is too detailed; and next, because I know my husband and he would never do anything like that." I insisted that I was not lying, and she was very firm about her stand. I got up, left the room, and went to the car crying. I called my best friend and told her what happened, and she was able to calm me down. My husband came to me and said, "We can leave now if you want to. We don't have to do this anymore." I said I was ready and went back to get our things. The pastor's wife asked me, "If my husband did this to you, then why didn't you tell me? Why did you keep coming to church?" "I came back to church for God because He didn't tell me to leave at that point. I was also working in the preschool alone with no subs. I didn't tell you because it wasn't my job to tell you and because I didn't know how to tell you that your husband sexually assaulted me. Besides, with your reaction now, it doesn't matter anymore if I told you or not," I said with so much frustration, then walked away. Before we left, we also made clear that we were not going back to church anymore.

The pastor begged us to let him and the church give us a proper sendoff, only because he wanted to cover his tracks. He was worried that people would wonder why I would just walk away like that, considering I was the praise and worship leader, and very well known and loved in the church. We told him that we didn't need a proper sendoff, walked out, and never talked to him again.

Rumors started to spread around on why we left the church. He told all the leaders that we left because he went to give me a hug and his hand grazed my bottom and that I lied about him sexually assaulting me. I ended up telling the leaders who wanted to know the truth on why I left the church. They were shocked, and they told me all the nasty things he and his wife said about me. I got so mad that before I left the state, I went to the police station and filed a sexual assault case against him. We only had three more weeks left in the state when I filed it. Yes, I know it was a bit late, but 'better late than never,' right? Well, the police told me they would have another office contact me once the file was processed. However, by the time we moved, I forgot about the filing. Besides, I was already across the country when they called to see if I wanted to proceed with the case. I told them to drop it because my husband was being shipped out to sea, and I had no one to take care of my kids. I also didn't have the funds to fly back and forth for a court hearing. I then asked them, "What took so long for you to file and contact me?" It turned out that someone had lost my file on their desk under a bunch of other files.

Some may say he lucked out. Thinking about it now, I believe he got a pass from God, not only for himself but from me as well. If they had found that case, I wouldn't be here today telling you my story. So, in a way, yes, I am very grateful.

As to the pastor, he is still out there in his pastoral role. I was grieved until now, and honestly, I feel that he should be in prison. Yet, God has a greater purpose. He wants me to be free from that bondage. He wants me to have the final victory. I do feel victorious.

Reflections

•Have you been so afraid to tell anyone about abuse that has happened to you? If so, what is stopping you?

Chapter 5
Questioning My Sanity

Not even a year has gone by, and I had a mind-blowing situation again. Yes, you read that right. We moved back home, and I thought it was going to be more than exciting to be with family once again. After healing from what I've been through with the pastor, I thought everything was going to be okay. I was wrong.

A week before Christmas, I let one of my cousins stay with me in my home. We became very close since we moved back. My husband and I bought a home in the same neighborhood where my family lived. These family members had to sell their home to move to another state, and my cousin wanted to stay. He asked if he could stay with me until he could save up for his own place. Incidentally, my husband was out at sea at that time. He was on the ship for work, so I emailed him, and he agreed that he could stay. He was living with us for almost a week, and on Christmas day my world changed again.

It was the morning of December 25. I went out for breakfast with my husband's family, after which I did my rounds of each family member's home. After a full day of running around, I finally got home and sent my kids to bed. My kids fell asleep pretty fast, so I decided to lie in bed and watch the Hallmark channel. My cousin came to the door asking me what I was watching, and I invited him to come in and watch if he wanted. He sat at the end of the bed on the opposite side of me. As we were watching the movie, I started to doze off to sleep. Next thing I knew my phone was ringing and it awakened me. I answered the phone, and I started talking to my friend about life and asking how each other's Christmas went. After being on the phone for about twenty minutes, I got off and looked over. Surprisingly, my cousin was still watching the movie, so I continued to watch the rest of it with him.

We talked about the movie after it was over. He said he liked it. I then asked him why he didn't have a girlfriend. He said, "I just haven't found the right one." He then went on talking about his ex and how they have been talking on and off, and how he missed her. "Is it weird that I still have her picture saved on my phone?" he asked. I told him that there are a lot of people who still have pictures of their ex's stashed somewhere.

The conversation started to get a little intense. He started talking about how he likes girls in panties rather than thongs. We started laughing and cracking jokes. He went on with a joke that he will slap me, and I told him I will slap him back. So, he came over and slapped me, and I did the same thing to him. He then started to tickle me, and since I am a very ticklish person, I ended up laughing and yelling "stop" at the same time. Suddenly, I got this bad feeling in my stomach. "Okay, hurry up and get him off before something weird happens," I began to tell myself in my mind. Just as I had that thought, BAM he kissed me on the lips. I pushed him away and said, "What the hell are you doing?" "I don't know. I'm sorry," he replied in shock.

I was in such disbelief as I sat there on my bed, trying to figure out what happened. The fact that I am married and we are cousins made me feel more sick and disgusted. I started to sweat and feel nauseous. I just sat there in dead silence for about ten minutes, thinking how to deal with the situation. We lived in the same house, and I didn't know how to proceed from there. "How will I even look at him? I can't lock myself in my own room each time he is around." These thoughts played in my mind over and over again, until I finally built up the courage to knock on his bedroom door.

The hallway seemed longer as I slowly inched my way to his room. I knocked on the door, and he let me in. "Do you think we can talk about what just happened?" I asked him. "Yes, let me finish taking my contacts out, and I'll be there in a minute," he said. I shut the door and walked back to my room. Five minutes later he was in my room.

We sat across from one another because he couldn't really see without his contacts. I told him that what happened cannot and will not ever happen again. He agreed with me, and I then asked him why he would even do something like that or what would make him think that it's okay. "I don't know; it just happened, and I don't know why," he answered. I felt this gut feeling in my stomach that there was more to this story, so I took a deep breath and asked, "Do you have feelings for me?"

He froze as he looked at me. "I can't answer that question," he said. I asked him why but all he told me was to ask a different question. "Do you feel like you like me or something?" I asked, rephrasing my question. He still didn't answer. I felt like I was talking to a brick, so I said, "Look at me in the face and tell me the truth." After a long silence, he finally opened his mouth and said, "Yes." I was shocked. "How long have you felt this way?" I asked curiously. "For a few weeks now," he said. "So, even before you moved into my home with not only me but with my children?" I clarified. I began to freak out, asking myself how and why and what in the hell was he thinking. I calmed myself down and slowly spoke to him. I grabbed his face and said, "Look at me." He refused to, so I ended the conversation right there. He finally looked at me and apologized. "I have been trying to get over my feelings for you, but it's been hard," he said. I reminded him how very inappropriate that was. He moved closer to me and said, "I know." I backed up and said, "What are you doing?" "Nothing," he whispered but continued to move closer to me. I told him to stop acting weird. He then started to kiss my neck, and I

tried to push him off. "Please stop. This is not okay."
He then got on top of me with all his body weight. I
tried to get him off as I kept saying, "Please, don't do
this." He went down to kiss me. I screamed and cried,
"Please stop. I love my husband." He then snapped out
of it and said, "Oh my God. I'm so sorry. I'm so sorry.
He walked into his room and shut the door while I laid
there and cried.

"How can he do this to me? We are family. He is my
cousin, and we were supposed to be close. How can he
do this to my husband?" I asked myself. "Did I do
this?" I further thought. "This is my fault. I should have
never let him stay here." I got up and went to the
bathroom to wash my face and clean myself up.
Thoughts came rushing to me unstoppably: "What do I
do now? What do I tell my husband? Why did he do

such a thing?" My mind was all over the place. Then it hit me that he has guns, which made it worse for me.

I was still awake when I heard him get up for work. I pretended that I was asleep and got out of bed once I heard the door shut. I tried to shift my mind to mommy mode, but it was very hard. Thoughts of what happened the night before were still taunting me, plus I felt woozy from barely having any sleep. Dazed and tired as I was, my heart leaped when I heard someone unlocking the back door. It was my cousin. He looked like he has not slept in weeks. He said "hey" and walked straight upstairs as if nothing happened between us.

"How can he pretend that last night didn't happen when he sexually assaulted me and forced himself on me?" I asked myself perplexed. I decided to go upstairs and knock on his door. "We need to talk," I said. "I am not feeling good, and I don't want to talk about last night. It is making me feel sicker," he responded. "I don't remember anything at all. All I remember was you yelling that you love your husband and me getting off you. Everything before that is a blur to me. I don't remember much," he added.

I stood there in total shock as I thought to myself, "Am I going crazy or did he go into a trance and came out of it from me yelling?" I snapped out of it and left it at that. That night, the kids and I stayed at my parents' place. I ended up telling them everything, and that I was scared and didn't know how to go back to my house with him living there. My dad told me I was not allowed to go back home until we get him out, and that I needed to call my uncle and aunt to let them know what their son did. At that point, my dad just wanted to go beat him up.

I sent my aunt a text message to call me after work, and she called that night. I told her everything, every single detail. She was shocked and mad at the same time. "I know he has been going through a rough patch, but this is crazy," she said. What she said next blew my mind and got my heart raging with fire. "God told me to talk to him about something like this happening. He told me to tell him that he better not catch some feelings or do anything stupid, but I didn't talk to him about it because I didn't feel the need." I got so quiet, and I said, "Well, Auntie, it did happen. "I was barely done with my sentence when she got an incoming call and told me that she will call me right back. She never did. I sent her another text message the next day explaining that her son needs to move out.

I left my parents' house the next day for an appointment when I realized that I forgot my paperwork at my house. I ended up going there scared and hoping that he wasn't around. I rushed and grabbed the papers, and I noticed that all his things were in the kitchen packed up in boxes. I raced to my car and drove off until I realized that I forgot a page in my room. I went back, and as I opened the door, he was there. "Hi," he said. I greeted him back but could not look at his face. He asked if we could talk and I told him I had to go to an appointment. Soon after I left, I got a text message from him asking if I can come back home so we can talk. I told him that it was not a good idea, but that I would call him after my meeting.

I got out of my appointment and called him. He answered the phone, and my heart felt like it was going 100 mph. "I'm sorry," he said. "It will never happen again. Can I stay, please? I have nowhere to go, and I love your house and feel comfortable with you and the kids." "No," I said. "You can't stay anymore." "I understand," he said. He moved out, and I moved back in. Not only did it feel like not my home anymore, but I felt scared to go to sleep in my own house.

A few days went by, and I still haven't heard from my uncle. I sent him a text message and asked him to call me. That day my phone rang. My heart pounded so hard it felt like it was coming out of my chest. I didn't know how to tell him about what had happened. I didn't know how he was going to take what I was about to tell him. All I knew was that he needed to know the truth. I finally picked up the phone and talked to him.

I asked him if he knew what happened and he said yes. I asked what he was told, and he said that my cousin and I exchanged a kiss.... that it was mutual. He said he didn't understand why cousins would kiss. I told him that was not true and went to tell him the whole story. As I was telling him, he kept saying, "Niece, I am so sorry. I can't believe that happened. I am so sorry." "I could just go off on him right now, but I'm going to call him and talk to him. I am just so sorry this has happened to you," he said. I thanked him and said, "I wish it never happened because my cousin and I have become close and I did want our relationship as cousins to stay the same, but now it can never be, and that makes me sad."

The next day, my uncle called me back and said that his son confessed everything to him. "I don't really have the words for you now, Latoya," he said. "I am sorry that this happened. I will call you again. Give me some time." A few days passed, and he called me. This time his voice sounded different. "My son told me some pretty disturbing things that you told him about what you and your husband do in the bedroom," he said. "I did what?" I asked in disbelief. "Man, I believe him because how would he know these things? They were pretty detailed, and I don't believe or think that he would make things up." By that time, I was mad. "Are you saying that it was my fault?" "Well, you basically got him horned up. I would never tell my cousin or anyone what my wife and I do in the bedroom," he said.

I got so upset and told him in between sobs, I wouldn't

do that, and I didn't tell him that, and even if I did tell him that, it still does not give him the right to sexually assault me." He kept pointing the blame back at me. I believed in my heart that truth will prevail, and that darkness will be exposed by the light. My husband will find out the truth about what really happened to me.

I was so hurt, angry, mad, sad, and I had so many emotions running through me after that conversation with my uncle. All I could do was cry. I called my sister bawling my eyes out and told her what our uncle just told me. She then calmed me down and said, "We all know the truth and that what he did was wrong." After hanging up, I just kept replaying that night in my head, and I started to question my sanity and myself. "Did I really tell him that? I don't remember that at all, but what if I really did tell him that? Is this really my fault?"

I couldn't even think straight anymore. I was all over the place in my thoughts. My husband had to leave the boat and come home because I needed him. I wasn't sleeping anymore.

I never talked to my uncle, auntie, and my cousin after that day. The funny thing is: my cousin changed his story so many times. First, he said it was mutual; then he admitted that what I said was true; then he told his dad that I told him sexual things that I do with my husband in bed. How can someone believe a person who has changed his story so many times? But then again, that's his son, so he will believe him over me. I should have seen it coming, right? I should have known because all my life no one wanted to believe me, except for a few people. It should not have been a big shock to me anymore. Yet, it still left a sting. Up to this day I still feel mad and hurt, but I no longer question my sanity. I woke up one day believing that what happened to me was not my fault. From that day until today, I wake up and live knowing that what happened that day changed my life, but I will not live with the burden that it was my fault.

Reflections

•What about you? When will you wake up and tell yourself not to question your sanity?

CONCLUSION
I Am The Story

From the time I was a kid until the time I reached the age of 25, I got pretty good at hiding any pain, concealing it from everybody. However, those last two sexual assaults finally got me. I thought that I could just forget it, as always, and continue to live my life as if I was okay. Not anymore. Once it all hit me, I turned away from God, my husband, family, and friends. I closed everyone off and went into a deep depression, one that I thought I would not be able to come out of. I looked good on the outside, but on the inside, I was so gone and just wanted to die.

I had so many suicidal thoughts. Yes, it was selfish to think that if I just die it will all be better. I was already dead on the inside; it didn't matter anymore if I died. I forgot how to be a mother. I ended up yelling at the kids when I tried playing with them. I could only focus for 30 minutes before I went back to sobbing on the inside.

I attempted to go to church and join the worship team. Everyone thought singing would make me feel better. However, it just made me feel worse. I wasn't true to myself anymore. I went to the altar call so many times, asking God, "Please, just get me out of this funk. Turn me back into the girl that had a fire burning spirit for Christ. Turn me back to the mom that I once was." I screamed from the inside for deliverance, and from the outside I made it look like everything within me was okay. I shut my husband out because I was so angry with him. Was it his fault? No, but I blamed him because he wasn't there to save me. I was so deep in the depression that no one or nothing could save me. And even when people told me that God was delivering me, I still felt the pain and said, "Yea, whatever that means." All I felt was anger inside when anyone told me anything about my past or anything about God. If He was really there for me, then why would he let this happen to me? Why didn't He protect me from all of these evil things that continue to happen to me? I was cursed, and no one can change this curse on me that just kept repeating itself in my life.

One Sunday, I finally said enough is enough. I went back to the altar and told God, "If you do not step in now and deliver me, I am going to take my life or taste and see how drugs would feel. I have been trying so hard to be strong and be an amazing mom, wife, sister, daughter, and friend, and I can't take it anymore. I'm broken, Lord, and I need to be healed." In those moments, I stood still and listened to what He had to say. This time I needed him more than ever. I remember Him saying, "Remember when I told you to write a book? And yet you have dismissed me. Get your life back on track and write your book. Wake up, My child. This is only the beginning of what I am about to do to you for you in your healing process. Let me help you. If you continue down this path, you will no longer be the child that I have called you to be, and you will be hopeless."

As I got up, I was mad because that's not what I wanted to hear. Yet, He still gave me what I needed. I woke up the next day, and I just knew that I should go to counseling. I needed help more than ever. I was desperate. Did I want to sit and talk to someone about my feelings? No, I didn't; but I had to still be there for my kids and my husband. I got myself into counseling and let me tell you that road was one of the hardest steps I had to take. I started to relive every chapter in this book. I broke down so many times I thought that each session would get better and better, but it got harder and harder to have to retell each story. I even missed some sessions because I was just tired of going through it. I didn't want to get up, and I didn't want to face what once was me. My counselor never pushed me or forced me to say or do anything. She listened and said all the things I needed to hear and what I didn't want to hear. Not only was she a counselor but she was all about God and for God. My faith started to get restored.

The process was not easy, but I decided I needed to go through it. At times I felt like giving up, and one day I really was going to give up, but my husband said some words to me that I will never forget. He said "I want my wife back. Where is she? I just want her back." Those words hit me so hard in the gut that I feared that if I quit he will give up on me. He and my kids were the only people left to fight for. So, I continued with my counseling sessions, and I kept going to church, praying and hearing and seeking God. I sought him at home on my face in tears. I sought him in the car when it was silent. I sought him when my kids were yelling and screaming, and I just wanted to yell and scream. I broke down the old me each and every day.

There were days when I would let the devil talk me out of being happy, and then I started to finally shut him up and tell myself positive things. I had to shut my old self up to bring back a new and refreshed me. What happened to me for many years are incidents that I cannot erase or take back, things I will never forget. Yet, to heal myself within, I had to learn how to forgive. Yes, I said forgive ... forgiving the people who did these nasty evil things. The longer I beat myself up to stay down in this depression, the more they robbed me of my life, my sanity, my dignity, my happiness, my hopes, my dreams, and my family.

Do I still get angry when I hear about them or see something on the internet or Facebook about them? Yes! But that's okay because that reminds me that I am still human, and I still get hurt, but I am living and walking in my freedom ... the very freedom they took from me. Guess what I took back this freedom from them.

Your road of sexual assault is your story. Never in a million years did I think that I would be sitting here still breathing and living and writing a book. Never did I think I would be able to sit here and say, "I forgive them for what they did to me". This has been a learning process for me, a process that has influenced me in my life.

As a mother, I have become very protective of my kids, not just my girls but also my son. I am very cautious about men coming up to them, and I have taught them to tell me right away if someone touches them in the wrong areas. I have encouraged them to tell me everything and to never keep a secret even when someone tells them to. When they go to stay with friends, I make sure that I know the parents and their backgrounds because you'll never know who or what type of people you are dealing with.

Moms and dads, please make sure that if you are dating someone or even before you date them, do a background check. Get to know who that person is before you introduce them to your children and family. You'll never know who you are truly dating until you get to know them and see them from the outside. You may think they are the greatest thing, but you won't know their true intentions until you know them deeply within.

To my teenage girls, being in love can really make you lose sight of things. I thought my ex-boyfriend loved me so much. I thought we would grow up to be together for a lifetime. But in the end, it wasn't about love; it was about sex. Don't lose sight of what love is. Remember to take the relationship slowly. Don't jump into sex because that's what you think will please him and get him to love you or like you more because in the end it will and can leave you broken hearted. I thought he loved me and that sex would make things better, but I wanted to stop, and he wanted to keep going. So please learn from what I went through and let this be an eye-opener to take things slow.

For so long I blocked out the truth with lies. I started to believe the lies that were spoken to me and the lies I told myself. I made myself block things out, and I would say, "Latoya, this never really happened to you as they told you. You can't believe that those things happened." I would wake up and never believe that those nasty dirty things happened to me. Why? Because if I believed that they never happened, then I could move on with life and I would be free, so I thought. But in reality, I wasn't free. The lies just changed me into someone I never want to go back to. I hated everything and everyone, and I never trusted anyone; but now I am a living, walking testimony, and how I choose to live is free within me.

How you choose to live is within you. I know that you may be saying, "Well, you never put any of them in prison. You never spoke up." I did. It may not be the way others would have spoken up, but it's the way I chose to speak up. I chose to speak up through writing this book, a book that talks about my journey from my old self to the new me.

Now I wake up happy, joyful, loving, and a much better person all around. I could be dead, but I am here. I want you to know that your life is valuable, and it is worth living. Don't count yourself out, and don't settle for less. Take it one day and one step at a time. Breathe and wake up and tell yourself that it's going to be okay. What happened to you does not define you or who you are, but it does get you ready to go and tell your story.

Shout it from the rooftop: "I am free, and I choose to be." Start a new chapter in your life. No matter how hard each chapter gets, no matter how much pain you feel, how much hate you feel, how much anger you feel, just write it down and tell those toxic emotions they can have the old you, but they cannot have the new person you are becoming.

I am free, and together we can all be.

Journal pages

You can begin to write your own story of breakthrough.

Journal page

Journal page